Contents

What is Judaism?

Jewish people go to the synagogue to pray to their God. Some Jewish people **worship** at home.

The Jewish star is called the Star of David. ▼

Can you find the Star of David on this synagogue?

Judaism

Izzi Howell

Franklin Watts
First published in paperback in Great Britain in 2021 by The Watts Publishing Group
Copyright © The Watts Publishing Group, 2018

Produced for Franklin Watts by
White-Thomson Publishing Ltd
www.wtpub.co.uk

ISBN: 978 1 4451 5967 6
10 9 8 7 6 5 4 3 2 1

Credits
Series Editor: Izzi Howell
Series Designer: Rocket Design (East Anglia) Ltd
Designer: Clare Nicholas
Literacy Consultant: Kate Ruttle
Religious Consultant: Dr Suzanne Owen, Leeds Trinity University

The publisher would like to thank the following for permission to reproduce their pictures: Getty: dnaveh *cover*, Noam Armonn *title page*, 16 and 18, BibleArtLibrary 6, Lesyy 7tr, Andia/UIG 8, stevenallan 9r, pushlama 10, RnDmS 11, Gerlow 12r and 23, Tara Walton/Toronto Star 13l, Eugene_Dudar 15t, Buccina Studios 15b, Katrina Wittkamp 17t; Shutterstock: Darren Whittingham 4l, Kletr 4r, margouillat photo 7tr, eriyalim 7bl, stockcreations 7br, eFesenko 9l and 22, natushm 12l and 13r, Donna Ellen Coleman 14, Silver Spiral Arts 17b, hadasit 19, Fotokon 20, Valentin Sama-Rojo 21.

Every attempt has been made to clear copyright. Should there be any inadvertent omission please apply to the publisher for rectification.

Printed in Dubai

MIX
Paper from
responsible sources
FSC® C104740

Franklin Watts
An imprint of
Hachette Children's Group
Part of The Watts Publishing Group
Carmelite House
50 Victoria Embankment
London EC4Y 0DZ

An Hachette UK Company
www.hachette.co.uk
www.franklinwatts.co.uk

All words in **bold** appear in the glossary on page 23.

Jewish people think that God looks after them. They worship God to thank him.

These Jewish men and boys are worshipping in a synagogue. They are wearing a Jewish hat called a kippah.

kippah

The Torah

The Torah is the Jewish **holy** book. There are stories in the Torah about God and people such as Moses. God told Moses to help Jewish people.

In one Torah story, Moses made a gap in the sea so that Jewish people could cross it safely. ▼

There are also rules in the Torah.
One rule is not to eat **pork**.

▼ Jewish people can eat beef (cow meat), chicken, lamb and fish.

beef

chicken

lamb

fish

Are there any foods that you don't eat? Why?

The synagogue

In the synagogue, Jewish people listen to the **rabbi** reading from the Torah.

▼ In some synagogues, the men and boys sit in a different place to the women and girls.

Holy Ark

rabbi

The Torah is written on **scrolls** of paper.
The scrolls are kept in a special cupboard
called the Holy Ark.

You can only touch
the Torah with a
metal stick. ▼

◀ The Holy Ark is covered
with a special cloth.

Praying

Jewish people pray together in the synagogue. They also say prayers at home.

▼ **This family is saying prayers before a meal.**

What do you do before a meal?

Jewish people pray to worship God. They thank him for good things and ask him for help.

▼ Jewish prayers are written in a language called Hebrew.

Hebrew writing

Shabbat

Shabbat is a day of rest. Jewish people celebrate Shabbat once a week. It begins when it gets dark on Friday evening. It ends on Saturday evening.

▼ Jewish people light candles and eat challah bread to celebrate Shabbat.

challah bread

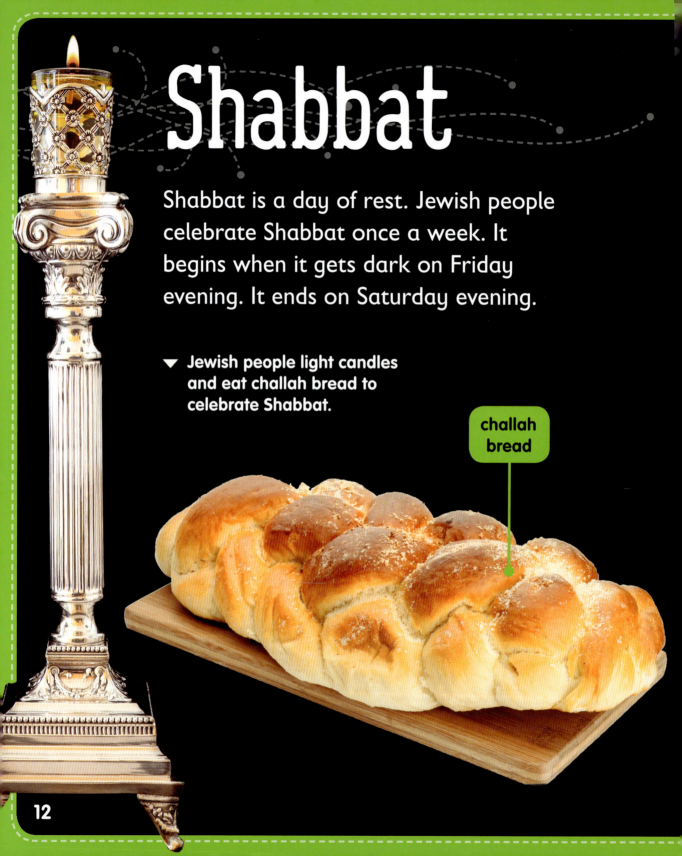

Jewish families eat dinner together on Friday night. Some Jewish families do not clean, cook or watch TV on Shabbat.

When do you have a special dinner with your family?

▼ This family is eating a Shabbat dinner together.

A Jewish life

Jewish children have a special **ceremony** when they are twelve or thirteen years old. They read from the Torah for the first time and say a prayer.

▼ The ceremony for a girl is called a bat mitzvah. It is called a bar mitzvah for a boy.

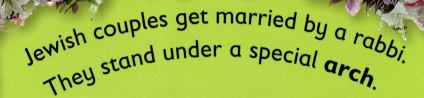

Jewish couples get married by a rabbi. They stand under a special **arch**.

Where can you see flowers at this wedding?

▲ At the end of the wedding, the man breaks a glass with his foot. There is a cloth wrapped around the glass so that the man doesn't cut his foot.

Hanukkah

Hanukkah is the Jewish festival of light. It lasts for eight days in November or December.

▼ Jewish people light a new candle on every night of Hanukkah. The candles are in a menorah candlestick.

When do you light candles?

menorah

Jewish people give each other presents during Hanukkah. Children play with dreidels (spinning tops).

▼ Children spin the dreidel to win chocolate coins.

Purim

Purim is a fun Jewish festival that usually happens in March. Jewish people celebrate by wearing **costumes** and masks.

▲ These children are wearing Purim costumes.

When do you wear a costume?

At Purim, Jewish people read about a woman called Esther. In her story, Esther saves the Jewish people from an **evil** man called Haman.

▲ Jewish people eat pastries filled with jam at Purim.

Around the world

Jewish people live in many places around the world. There are Jewish people in North America, Europe and Africa.

▼ These Jewish boys live in the country of Israel.

Jewish people like to spend time with each other. They study, worship and celebrate festivals together around the world.

▲ A girl lights the menorah at a Hanukkah celebration in Spain.

Quiz

Test how much you remember.

Check your answers on page 24.

1 What is the Torah?

2 Where is the Torah kept in a synagogue?

3 When does Shabbat begin?

4 What is a bar mitzvah?

5 How long does Hanukkah last?

6 Which food do Jewish people eat at Purim?

Glossary

arch – a curved structure

ceremony – a special event

costume – clothes that make you look like someone or something else

evil – very bad

holy – very important for a religion

pork – meat from a pig

rabbi – a Jewish religious leader

scrolls – a long roll of paper

worship – to show that you think a god is important by praying or doing something religious

Index

Answers:

1: The Jewish holy book; 2: The Holy Ark; 3: Friday evening; 4: A celebration for a Jewish boy when he is twelve or thirteen; 5: Eight days; 6: Pastries filled with jam

Teaching notes:

Children who are reading Bookband Gold or above should be able to enjoy this book with some independence. Other children will need more support. All children may benefit from help pronouncing unfamiliar words linked to Judaism.

Before you share the book:

- Are any of the children in your class Jewish? Can they tell you about their experiences and understanding?
- Talk together about the religions of other children. What is the same/what is different from Jewish children's experiences?

While you share the book:

- Help children to read some of the more unfamiliar words and concepts.
- Discuss the fact many of the stories in the Torah are also found in the Christian Bible.

- Talk about the questions. Encourage children of different faiths or no faith to share their own answers.
- Talk about the pictures. Help children to identify who or what the captions refer to: how is the synagogue the same as or different to other places of worship (p4)? What might a rabbi do in a synagogue (p8)? How do you move on to the next page when you're reading from a scroll like the Torah (p9)? How many candles fit into a menorah candlestick (p16)?

After you have shared the book:

- Find out more about other stories from the Torah. Are they the same or different from similar stories the children already know?
- Arrange to take the children to visit a synagogue. Ask them to look for things mentioned or shown in the book.
- Work through the free activity sheets from our Teacher Zone at www.hachettechildrens.co.uk